Patchwork

A beginner's step-by-step guide to patterns
and techniques

CHARLOTTE GERLINGS

FOX CHAPEL
PUBLISHING

To Thelma M. Nye, craft editor at B. T. Batsford Ltd for over thirty years and
friend and advisor to many grateful authors and designers.

Copyright © 2011, 2012 Arcturus Publishing Limited.

First Published in the United Kingdom by Arcturus Publishing Limited, 2011.
First published in North America in 2012, revised, by Fox Chapel Publishing, 1970 Broad Street, East Petersburg, PA 17520.

ISBN 978-1-56523-685-1

Front cover photo by kind permission of Vanessa Koble
With thanks to Martha Preston for permission to photograph her patchwork for the back cover
Color wheel, back cover: Shutterstock

Illustrated by David Woodroffe

Library of Congress Cataloging-in-Publication Data

Gerlings, Charlotte.
 Patchwork / Charlotte Gerlings. -- 6th
   p. cm. -- (Craft workbooks)
 ISBN 978-1-56523-685-1
 1. Patchwork--Patterns. 2. Patchwork quilts. I. Title.
 TT835.G3322 2011
 746.46--dc23
                2011024130

Fox Chapel Publishing, or to find a retailer near you, call toll-free 800-457-9112 or visit us at *www.FoxChapelPublishing.com*.

Note to Authors: We are always looking for talented authors to write new books. Please send a brief letter
describing your idea to Acquisition Editor, 1970 Broad Street, East Petersburg, PA 17520.

Printed in China
First printing

Because working with fabric and other materials inherently includes the risk of injury and damage, this book cannot guarantee that creating the projects in this
book is safe for everyone. For this reason, this book is sold without warranties or guarantees of any kind, expressed or implied, and the publisher and the author
disclaim any liability for any injuries, losses, or damages caused in any way by the content of this book or the reader's use of the tools needed to complete
the projects presented here. The publisher and the author urge all readers to thoroughly review each project and to understand the use of all tools before
beginning any project.

CONTENTS

INTRODUCTION

Patchwork is a craft for people of all ages. There is such a variety of shapes and designs to choose from that everyone should find something to suit their tastes and capabilities. Like other titles in the series, this book has been prepared with the beginner in mind, taking them through the methods and techniques in easy stages. However, it also features plenty of templates and patterns to inspire more experienced stitchers to try their hands, perhaps at a dazzling Mennonite star or delicate Hawaiian appliqué.

You don't have to make an entire quilt all at once. Piece together just one intricate block of patchwork and if you go no further, you have a unique cushion cover or a decorative panel for the side of a tote bag. Using scraps, young children can start on a simple cover for a doll's bed or cheerful padded pot holders; the basic four- or nine-piece block makes an easy introduction for them. Although this book was originally published in the UK, the technical terms and phrases throughout have been revised with a US audience in mind.

Although strongly associated now with North America, it was the ingenuity of European immigrants that laid the foundations of patchwork, quilting and appliqué there. As the newcomers arrived and spread westwards, their expertise and patterns travelled along with them. The same diamond-pieced pattern named *Ship's Wheel* in Massachusetts became *Harvest Sun* in the Midwest where there was no ocean but acre upon acre of cornfields. The most famous pattern of all, *Log Cabin,* says everything about the pioneering lifestyle of the early settlers.

Making the most of scarce resources, warm bed covers were cleverly pieced and quilted in styles that were regularly handed down to younger generations of women by their mothers and grandmothers. The bridal quilt represented the peak of a young woman's stitching skills, after she had spent so much of her girlhood perfecting them.

As people grew more affluent, they bought manufactured items rather than making them at home. But this meant they could also buy brand new fabrics in larger quantities, and so quiltmaking— including hand stitching and appliqué—developed as a decorative art and spread back to Europe once again. The traditional designs with evocative names like *Birds in the Air*, *Prairie Queen* and *Drunkard's Path* have been preserved to this day and continue to be worked expertly by enthusiastic quilters all over the world.

PART ONE:
EQUIPMENT AND MATERIALS

TEMPLATES

Templates are used for cutting out multiple pattern pieces.

Made from metal, plastic or cardboard, templates may be bought readymade from needlecraft suppliers, or cut out carefully at home from graph paper stuck on to strong cardboard or acetate. There are three types (arrows indicate fabric grain direction, see p.8):

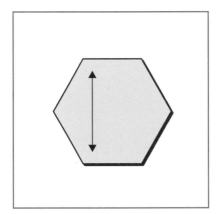

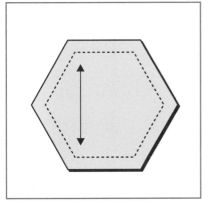

1 Exact size and shape of the finished patch—use when cutting papers for hand sewing (p. 20). No seam allowance, cut fabric with ¼ in [6 mm] extra all round.

2 Incorporates the shape *and* a ¼ in [6 mm] seam allowance— use when cutting fabric for machine sewing.

3 Inner margin marks the actual patch size; outer margin adds seam allowance. Window helps to center a motif.

A **Sharps needles** for general sewing with standard cotton or polyester thread; **betweens** for fine stitching and quilting.

B Colored glass- or plastic-headed **pins** are easier to see and handle.

C Medium thickness (No 50) cotton **thread** for hand sewing patchwork. A stronger cotton (No 40) or cotton/polyester mix should be used for machine sewing. Thread up with the free end straight off the spool and not only will it pass more easily through the needle's eye, it won't tangle while you work.

D To hand sew more quickly and smoothly, draw your thread across a block of **beeswax**. Wax treatment combats high humidity and kills static electricity from synthetics.

E A **thimble** is necessary for pushing needles through several layers of fabric at once. Some quilters wear one on each hand.

F A **seam ripper** for removing machine stitching. Use with care as it is all too easy to pierce surrounding fabric.

G **Dressmaking shears** have asymmetric handles and long blades for cutting smoothly through fabric at a low angle on a flat surface. Do not allow anyone—including yourself—to dull them by cutting paper, cardboard, string or sticky tape.

H **Embroidery scissors** for precision cutting. The blades are 1.25–4 in [3–10 cm] in length and sharply pointed.

I **Craft knife** for cutting templates. Use in conjunction with a self-healing cutting mat (**J**) and metal straight edge (**K**). Change blades frequently.

L A **rotary cutter** rapidly cuts strips and several layers of fabric at once. Change blades frequently. A locking mechanism retracts the blade for safety. Use in conjunction with a cutting mat (**J**) and rotary ruler that has straight and diagonal markings (see p. 18).

M **Acrylic dressmaker's ruler** marked with a grid to help you draw accurate templates.

N **Ruler** marked in centimeters and inches.

O **Gauge** fitted with a sliding marker that allows you to set it on a fixed measurement.

P **Pair of compasses** for drawing curved templates.

Q **Protractor** for measuring angles of templates.

R **Quilter's fabric-marking pencil**

S **Dressmaker's chalk pencil with brush end**

T **Graph paper** for drawing accurate templates and drafting patterns.

U **Spray adhesive** for sticking paper templates to cardboard.

V **Glue stick** for temporarily positioning appliqué shapes. Test on scrap fabric first.

W **Sewing machine**

X **Iron**

FABRIC

Fabrics consist of natural or man-made fibers, often mixed to combine their best qualities.

Woven fabric

Every woven fabric belongs to one of three types:

1 Plain weave Alternate warp (lengthwise) threads go over one and under one of the weft (crosswise) threads. Calico, taffeta and poplin are familiar examples.

2 Twill weave Interlaces warp and weft threads over and under two or more threads progressively, to produce a clear diagonal pattern on hardwearing fabrics such as denim or gabardine.

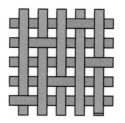

3 Satin weave A smooth, compact surface created by long silky floats that leave no weft visible; the reverse is matt. The glossy surface tends to snag.

Shrinkage

The tighter the weave, the less likely a fabric is to shrink during or after manufacture. The shop label should say if a fabric is pre-shrunk. *If it is not, you must do it yourself before cutting out.* Immerse in plain hot water for half an hour. This also reveals any problems with color fastness.

The grain

The grain of a fabric is the direction in which the warp and weft threads lie. The warp runs lengthwise, parallel to the selvage; this is the *lengthwise grain*. The weft follows the *crosswise grain*, at right angles to the selvage.

The bias

Bias lies along any diagonal line between lengthwise and crosswise grains. The angle of 45 degrees provides maximum stretch. Bias strips are often used for piping and binding edges because of their flexibility on curves and corners.

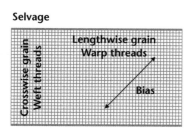

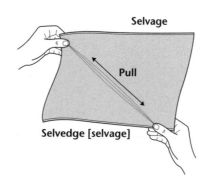

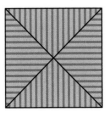 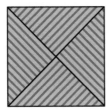 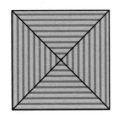

Texture comes from the weave of a fabric. It also depends whether the cloth has a distinct nap or pile, like velvet or corduroy (see left), which can be brushed in different directions. You can show ingenuity with texture, even when the patches are identical.

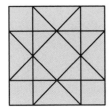 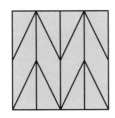 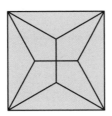

Pattern-making is limitless with patchwork. Try the templates in various combinations. Striped and checked fabrics can be used most effectively, and you can play around with the scale of prints too.

The color wheel *(see rear cover)* provides a lesson in color harmonies. Red, yellow and blue are the primary colors. The secondary colors are green, orange and purple from mixtures of the primaries. The tertiary colors lie between the primaries and secondaries. Colors directly opposite each other on the circle are complementary and make the most vibrant combinations. Those next to each other are called analogous. Colors from red to yellow-green occupy the warm spectrum, while from green to red-purple they are described as cool.

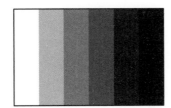

1 Color value refers to the relative lightness or darkness of a color.

2 These values are significantly affected by adjoining colors.

Batting and lining or backing

Batting is the soft fibrous material sandwiched for warmth between the top of a quilt and the lining fabric. It may be totally synthetic, like polyester, or consist of natural fibers, such as wool or cotton, mixed with polyester.

Lining—with or without batting—neatens and strengthens a quilt. Pre-shrunk dress-weight cotton is ideal.

Fat quarters

A fat quarter means getting larger pieces of fabric than possible from a standard quarter of a yard, including strips twice as long on the lengthwise grain. If you hav difficulty finding fat quarters at your local retailers, they are readily available online.

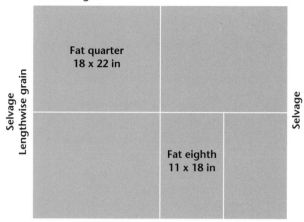

Crosswise grain

Selvage

Lengthwise grain

Fat quarter
18 x 22 in

Fat eighth
11 x 18 in

Selvage

One yard of fabric, 36 x 44 in

Regular quarter yard, 9 x 44 in

Calculating quantities

The standard widths for fabric are 36, 44–45 and 54 in [90, 115 and 150 cm]. Dress-weight fabric is usually 44–45 in [115 cm]; muslin and interfacings come in 36 in [90 cm] widths.

Study your pattern. How many different templates does it use? How many patches of each shape? Before calculating, take 2 in [5 cm] off the width for shrinkage and removal of selvages. *Be sure to include seam allowances.*

1 See how many times a template fits into the fabric width and divide that number into the total number of patches required of that particular shape.

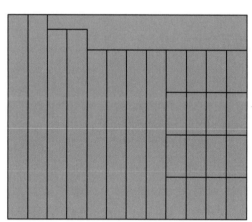

2 Do the same for the number of lengthwise strips for borders and sashing (p. 26–7).

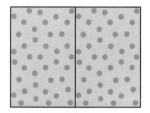

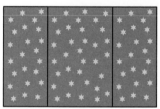

3 For linings, be prepared to piece together two or three widths, depending on the quilt size.

To estimate the length of fabric needed after 1 and 2, divide the total number of patches by the number in a single width and multiply the result by the width of the template.

An economical cutting plan takes straight strips from one edge of the fabric and irregular shapes from the other. Bias-binding or piping around the edges uses strips cut on the diagonal, which will lead to some wastage.

THE SEWING MACHINE

A well-built sewing machine will give decades of service so long as it is properly used and maintained.

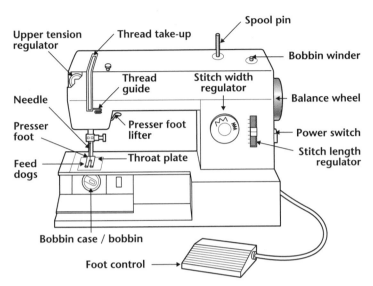

- Upper tension regulator
- Thread take-up
- Spool pin
- Bobbin winder
- Thread guide
- Stitch width regulator
- Needle
- Balance wheel
- Presser foot
- Presser foot lifter
- Power switch
- Stitch length regulator
- Feed dogs
- Throat plate
- Bobbin case / bobbin
- Foot control

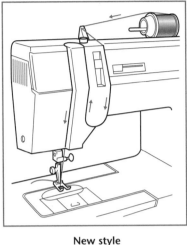
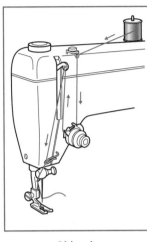

New style   **Old style**

Regularly clear lint from the feed dogs and bobbin area with a small brush. Oil the machine only according to the maker's instructions. Avoid bent needles by raising the needle high before removing work and don't drag on it while stitching. Always raise the presser foot while threading the machine, and lower it when you put the machine away. *Switch power off at the wall before disconnecting any plugs or attempting cleaning or repairs.*

Newer-style machines incorporate tension discs, thread guides and the take-up lever inside their casings, avoiding various steps involved with threading older models. Be aware that some needles thread from front to back and some from left to right. Incorrect threading is probably responsible for more beginners' problems than any other factor. Always consult the manufacturer's manual for instructions on use and maintenance. If you have no printed instructions, search for your make and model on the internet, where a huge range of manuals are available.

Four machine feet that form a basic kit for quilters:

1 Straight-stitch The general purpose presser foot that comes ready to use on most machines.

2 Zigzag Has a horizontal slot to allow for the swing of the needle as it forms a zigzag with the thread.

3 Zipper Used to insert zippers and cording, or anywhere that the stitch line needs to run close. The foot can slide to left or right, the needle operating in the tiny notch between the foot and the zipper.

4 Walking/quilting Uses teeth to feed upper and lower layers of fabric together evenly and avoid bunching.

GRAPH PAPER   **Square grid**

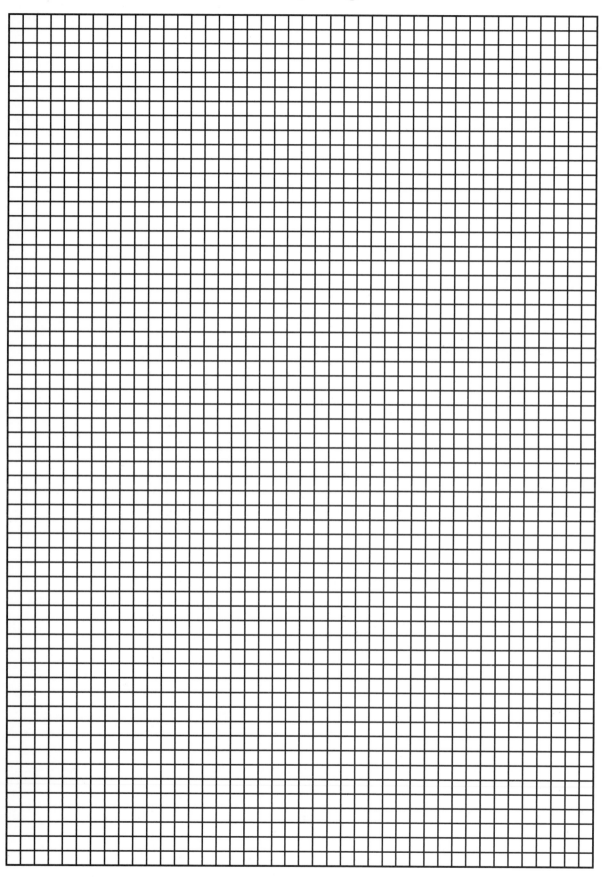

GRAPH PAPER   Isometric

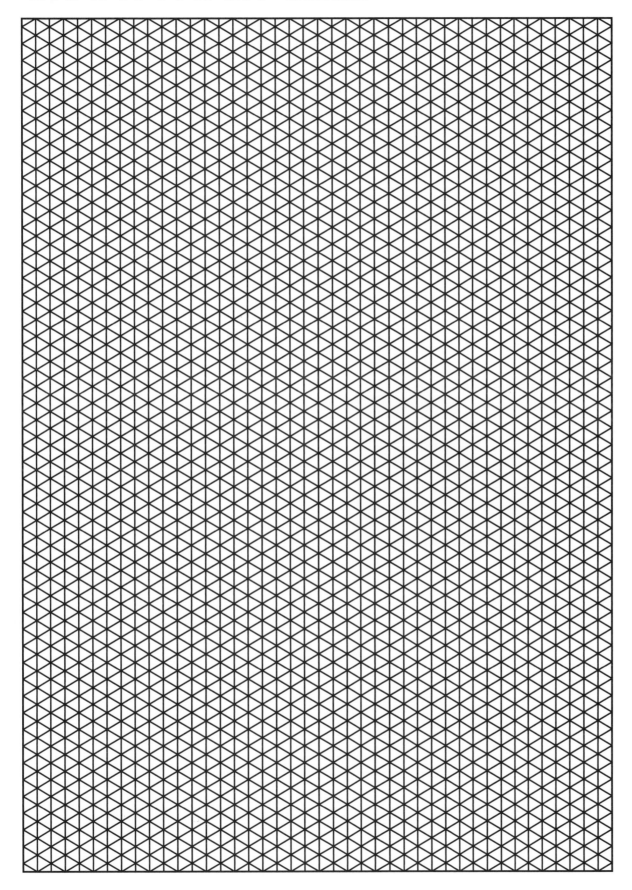

CURVED TEMPLATES

Shell

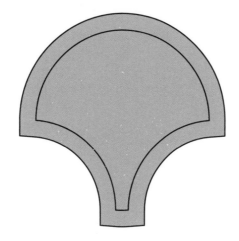

Drunkard's path

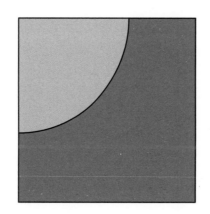

Double axehead

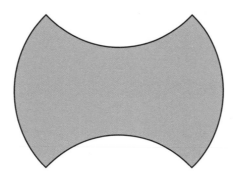

PART TWO:
PIECED PATCHWORK METHODS AND TECHNIQUES

Before undertaking a full-sized quilt or wall hanging, try something smaller for your first attempt at patchwork. Table toppers, place mats, pillow covers and cot quilts are all good starter projects.

GRAPHS

Choose a design in scale with the finished piece. A big repeat pattern is clearly not suitable for a baby's quilt but at the same time, don't make something with scores of tiny patches that takes too long to finish.

Graph paper, squared (p. 12) and isometric (p. 13), will serve for drafting out your overall pattern, and then for drawing individual patches to the precise shape and size you require. Decide which of the three types of template you need (p. 5) depending on whether you are cutting papers, hand or machine sewing.

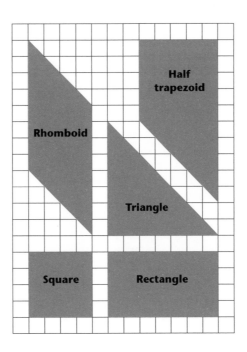

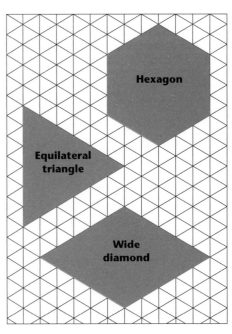

MAKING TEMPLATES

Cut out the shapes carefully from the graph paper because these will form your templates. The slightest inaccuracy now becomes a bigger problem at the sewing stage.

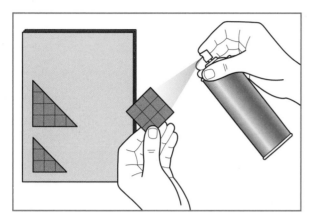

1 With spray adhesive, glue each shape to a sheet of mounting board or acetate.

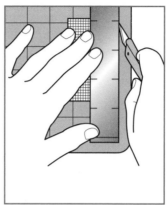

2 Cut out the templates with a sharp craft knife and metal straight edge. Keep fingers clear of the blade.

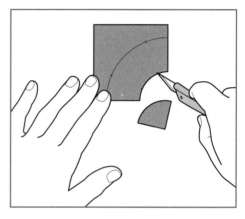

3 Cut notches into any curved templates. Notches are later marked on the fabric to help match pieces when joining.

Label the templates with an arrow for grain direction (p. 5) and "This way up" if there is any risk of confusion. Also, make a note on them of how many of each shape you need, and from which fabric. Detailed preparation saves time.

Medium-grade sandpaper can be used for templates. It is perfect for short-term projects and grips the fabric well when marking out. A whole sheet of sandpaper placed under slippery fabric holds it steady while tracing.

STANDARD SHAPES

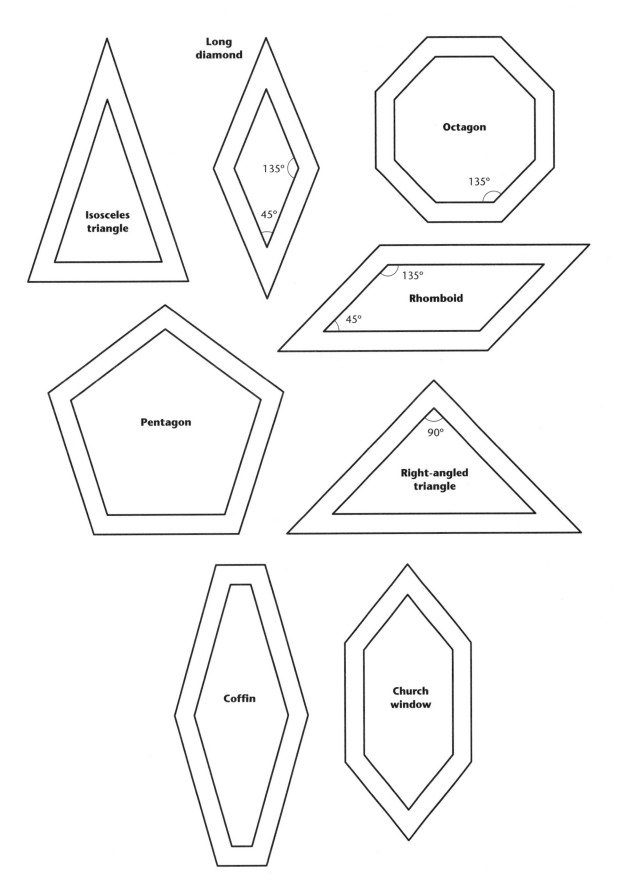

Long diamond

135°

45°

Octagon

135°

Isosceles triangle

Rhomboid

135°

45°

Pentagon

Right-angled triangle

90°

Coffin

Church window

CUTTING SHAPES FROM FABRIC

With a sharp pencil, mark patchwork shapes on the wrong side (WS) of your fabric, starting with any border strips or sashing (pp. 26–7). Cut long pieces with the grain and curved ones on the bias.

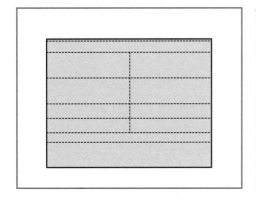

1 Include a ¼ in [6 mm] seam allowance on strips. For accuracy, use a straight edge squared up with a dressmaker's ruler.

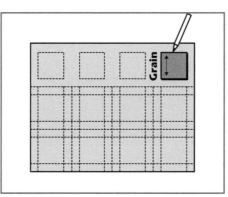

2 Templates for hand sewing are marked out with a ¼ in [6 mm] margin. With practice, you can do this by eye.

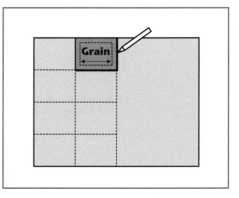

3 Templates for machine sewing include seam allowances and need no margins. However, accurate cutting is essential.

Using a rotary cutter and ruler

Remember to include a ¼ in [6 mm] seam allowance. Spray-starch and press the main strips before cutting further.

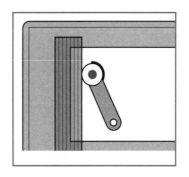

1 Cutting plain strips

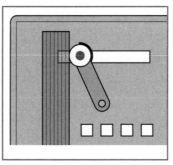

2 Cutting squares

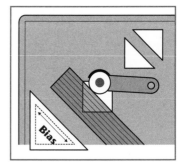

3 Cutting right-angled triangles

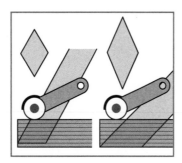

4 Cutting diamonds

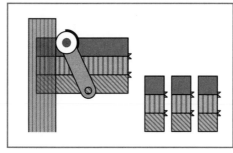

5 Cutting sewn strips

SEMINOLE PATCHWORK

Strip-pieced Seminole—often used for decorative borders—is named after the American Indians of Southern Florida, whose vibrant machine-sewn patchwork developed around 1920.

Use pre-shrunk, solid-color fabric for Seminole. Remove the selvages and cut into strips; lightly spray-starch and press. After sewing, press seams to one side, preferably toward darker fabrics to prevent show-through. Cut into more strips.

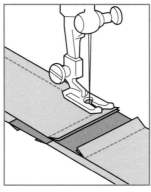

1 Arrange pieced strips into the desired pattern.

2 Sew strips together, first in pairs; then continue piecing until the band is completed.

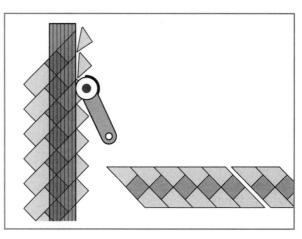

3 Trim top and bottom edges with ¼ in [6 mm] seam allowance.

Border designs

Bold, clear colors give the best results. Three or four colors make a simple pattern look really intricate.

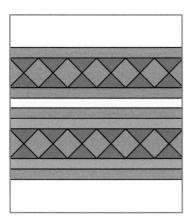

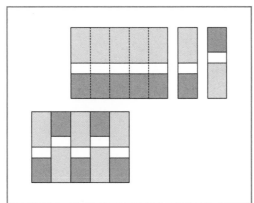

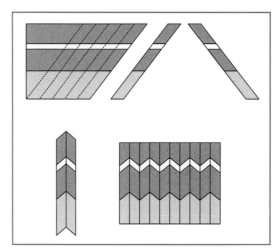

1 Sew one or more straight-grain edging strips to the main band for different effects.

2 Sew three colors together in varying widths. Cut, and reverse alternate strips.

3 Make a zigzag pattern with strips cut at an angle of 45 degrees. Take care not to stretch when sewing.

ENGLISH PATCHWORK

One-shape hexagon patchwork is traditionally associated with English hand-sewn designs, made from cotton fabric folded neatly over backing papers.

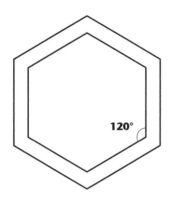

The inner hexagon of this window gives the finished patch size and is also a template for the papers (p. 5); cut them from old magazine or catalogue pages. Use the outer margin of the window template for cutting out the patch plus seam allowance. Alternatively, pin a paper to the fabric first and cut round it with ¼ in [6 mm] allowance.

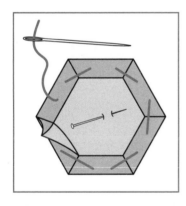

1 Pin paper to fabric. Folding fabric over as you go, baste through fabric and paper, right around the patch. This holds everything in place until final stitching is done. Prepare all hexagons this way.

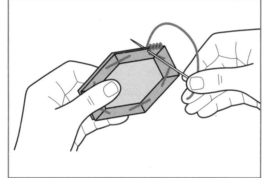

2 Join patches by placing RS together and oversew one side neatly from corner to corner. Keep stitches small, just catching the fold of fabric each time.

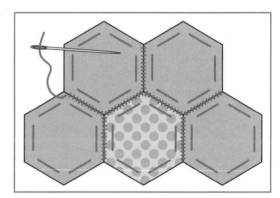

3 Make a single rosette by joining six hexagons around a central one. Double and treble rosettes are formed by adding further rings of patches. Do not break off your thread but go as far as you can with one length. Basting and papers stay in position until the final stages of a project.

Hand-sewing stitches for patchwork

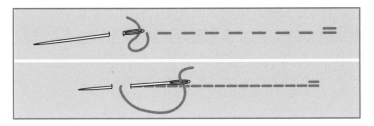

Running stitch (left) Secure thread with two small stitches. Push needle in and out of fabric evenly.

Back stitch (lower left) Start as for running stitch but go back over the first space. Needle out again at one stitch length ahead of last stitch made. Repeat, with needle back in at the point where previous stitch ends.

Oversewing or **whip stitch** Secure thread with two small stitches on the spot and proceed with neat diagonal stitches equally spaced. Sew from left to right or vice versa.

Slip stitch attaches a folded edge invisibly to a flat surface. Take up a few threads of flat fabric with your needle, enter fold and slide along inside before emerging to make the next stitch.

PROJECT: PLACE MAT

The mat features a single rosette stitched to plain foundation fabric. From the foundation fabric, cut two hexagons to the desired size of the mat, plus 3/8 in [1 cm] seam allowance. A third layer of non-woven interfacing is optional.

Calculate the rosette size and, from that, the size of a single hexagon. Follow the instructions for making a template (p. 16). Cut papers with the template and sew the rosette as shown opposite. Remove the basting and papers and press face down.

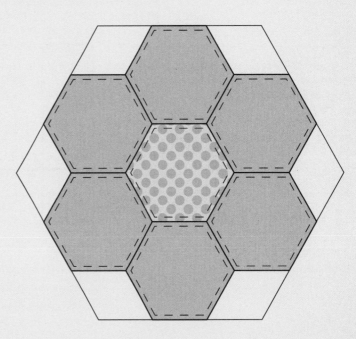

Pin and baste the rosette to the RS of one of the large hexagons. Attach it by slip stitching to the foundation fabric. Topstitch neatly round each hexagon for extra firmness. Use pearl embroidery thread for a decorative effect.

Pin and baste the two large hexagons RS together. Machine around five sides without sewing through the rosette. Clip corners, turn the mat RS out and slip stitch the remaining side closed. Press face down.

TO SEW BY HAND OR MACHINE?

Both methods are acceptable—it's a matter of personal preference. Hand sewing is slower but some processes, like folding sharp corners and setting in (p. 25), are easier. Machine sewing is quicker, and often stronger, but mistakes will involve careful use of a seam ripper.

Hand sewing without papers

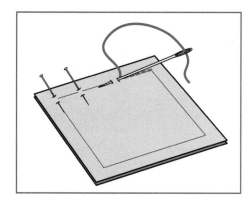

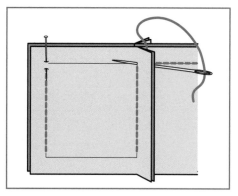

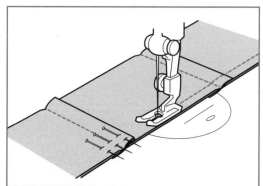

1 Pin patches RS together, matching the marked lines front and back. Sew small, even running stitches along the lines, starting and ending with a back stitch. Join several patches like this to form a row.

2 Join rows with running stitch. At each cross seam, do a back stitch as in 1. Needle through the seam allowance and make another back stitch. This ensures a neat join at each corner.

3 Press seams to one side, either toward darker fabrics to prevent show-through or to alternate sides to avoid bulk.

Piecing by machine

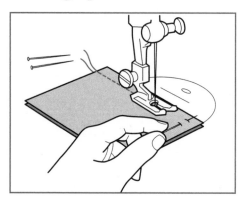

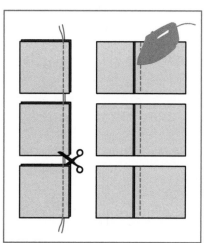

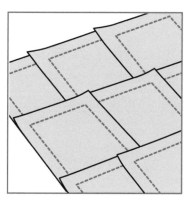

1 Pin patches RS together. In the absence of marked lines, stitch to a seam allowance set by the edge of the presser foot. Remove pins as you go.

2 Chain paired patches together to save time and thread. Cut apart and press seams to one side.

3 When joining rows, pin seam allowances in different directions to avoid bulk. Remove pins as you go.

JOINING TECHNIQUES

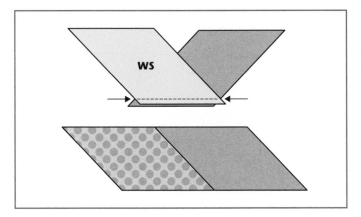

Offset seams Oblique-angled shapes such as rhomboids and diamonds should be offset when stitched together. When turned RS, they appear flush at the edges.

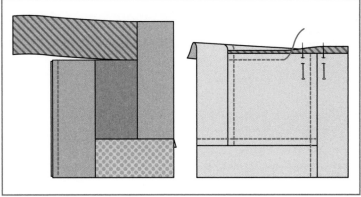

Joining right-angles To add the fourth strip around a central square: stitch halfway; open and pin the extended pieces to the new strip; complete the seam.

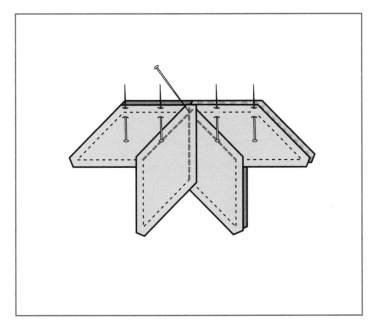

Eight-seam join To join two halves of an 8-point star: pin through the center of both halves where the stitching meets at a point. Pin the rest of the two halves together along the seam allowance and hand-stitch with care so points meet accurately at the center. Open flat and press all seams in one direction, twirling the center as for set-ins (p. 25).

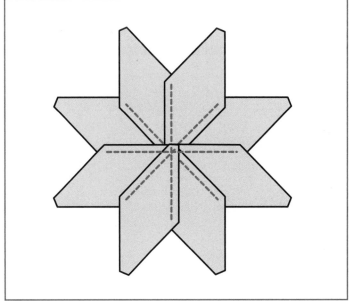

By machine Stitch the two halves together along the seam allowance, passing straight across the point of the topmost diamond. Open flat and press seams as they lie from the initial piecing.

BLOCKS

The block method of quilt construction is essentially American. Developed from early colonial days when the whole family slept under one huge quilt, manageable units were sewn separately and later assembled into an overall pattern.

Blocks are usually based on a grid; four-, five- and nine-patch blocks are among the most common. Their distinctive regional names commemorate people, places and events of the times.

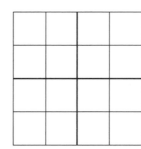 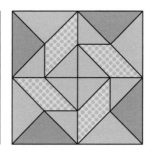

Windblown Square The number of pieces in any four-patch block is always divisible by four.

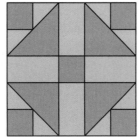

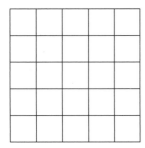

Grandmother's Choice Five-patch blocks are constructed on a grid of twenty-five squares.

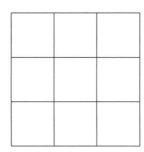 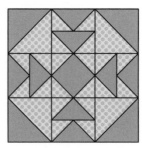

T-Block Nine-patch blocks are ideal for beginners and underlie many traditional patterns.

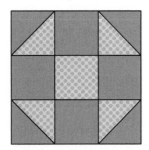

Shoo-fly (9-patch)

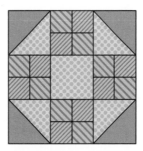

Prairie Queen (9-patch)

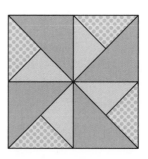

Whirlwind/Oh Susannah (4-patch)

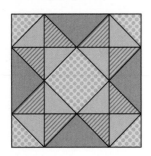

Old Tippecanoe (9-patch)

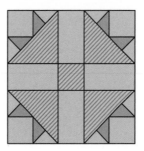

Cross and Crown (9-patch)

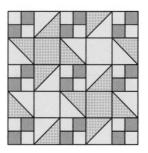

Milky Way (5-patch)

SETTING IN

Hand setting in

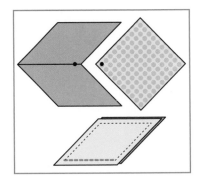

1 Setting in fits one piece into an angle formed by two others already joined. The seam on the first pair should end in a back stitch ¼ in [6 mm] from the edge.

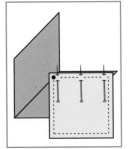

2 RS together, pin the new piece into the angle with corners matching (see dots). Stitch from the outer edge into the corner, do a back stitch but do not cut thread.

3 Pull new piece round to pin its adjacent side into the angle. Stitch from the back stitch to the outer edge of the join.

Machine setting in

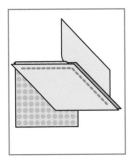

1 RS together, pin the new piece into the angle with corners matching. Machine stitch from the corner to the outer edge. Cut thread.

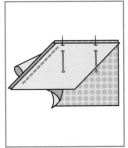

2 Pull new piece round to pin its adjacent side into the angle. Stitch from the corner to the outer edge of the join.

Sewing curved seams

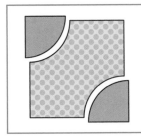  

1 Match notches (p. 16) on both pieces and pin RS together from the center outward, easing the fit as you go.

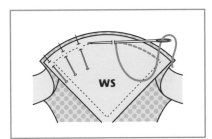

2 Starting and finishing with a back stitch, sew by hand or slowly by machine. Remove pins as you go.

Pressing hand and machine stitching

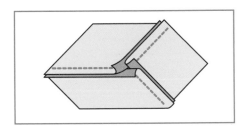

Hand-sewn set-ins should be twirled open before pressing to avoid bulk at the join. Press carefully on both sides.

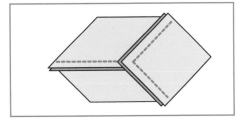

Machine-sewn set-in pieces are pressed toward the seam of the first pair, which is folded to one side. Press carefully on both sides.

Where possible, avoid setting in at right-angles by piecing a block in horizontal or vertical strips that can be joined with straight seams.

PUTTING BLOCKS TOGETHER

These sets demonstrate four principal ways of putting quilt blocks together.

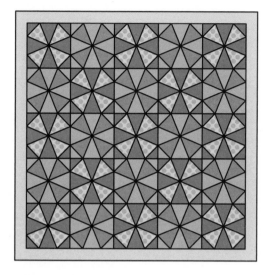

Edge to edge Blocks are joined directly to one another, often forming an intricate geometric pattern. A variation is to alternate pieced and plain blocks, increasing the patchwork area with no extra piecing.

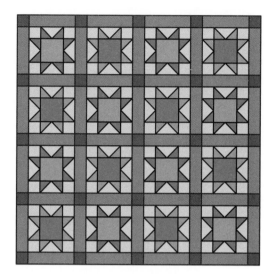

Sashing Also called latticing, where blocks are separated by narrow strips. Sashing may also be done in one direction only.

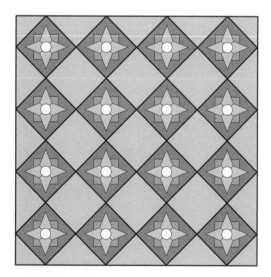

Diagonal Blocks are turned through 45 degrees and set on their points.

Strip Strips of alternating designs are sewn together; they may consist both of pieced work and plain or patterned fabric.

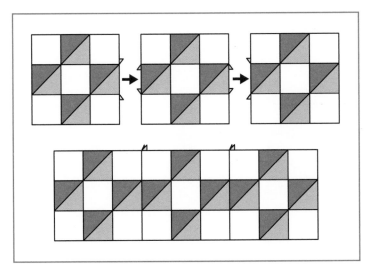

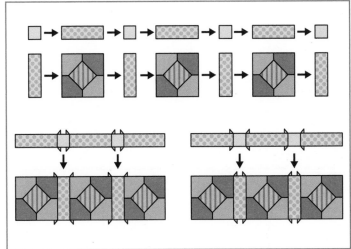

Joining edge to edge Blocks are joined to one another in rows. Each block is sewn, RS facing, to its neighbour with the normal ¼ in [6 mm] seam allowance. The allowances are pressed in different directions on adjacent rows.

Joining sashing This particular style uses contrasting squares (posts) at the intersections, so the sashing itself is pieced like a block. Seam allowances are pressed in opposite directions to avoid bulk.

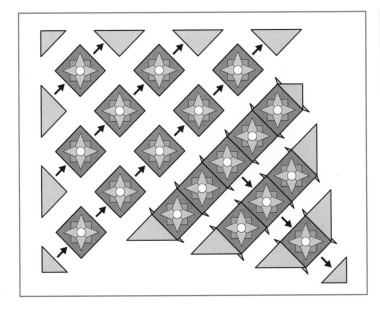

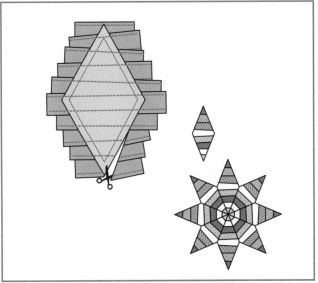

Joining diagonals The diagonal rows are squared off at the edges with half- and quarter-square pieces.

Stringing produces a totally new fabric from which other shapes and patterns may be created. It evolved from sewing narrow offcuts together at random. Today it is often used for a planned effect. Creative cutting and re-piecing can give kaleidoscopic results.

THE PATCHWORK QUILT

Whether the design is simple or complex, a quilt is a major project. Even one-piece patterns need a plan, especially with regard to the color scheme. Get hold of some graph paper (pp. 12–13) and make a few scale drawings. Even if you have set your heart on a certain pattern you still need to devise a border.

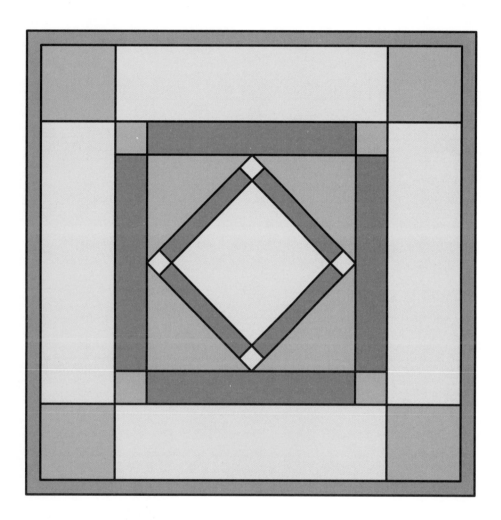

The plain-living Amish people emigrated from Europe and settled in the Americas, in the 1700s. This bold *Center Diamond* is one of their oldest designs. Large areas of plain fabric were quilted with tiny stitches (pp. 44–45), creating curled feathers, shells and stars to enliven the sober geometry.

An Amish-style block can be made any size you choose. It could easily be adapted to form one element of a pieced and plain pattern. And in Amish tradition, the colors could include burgundy, olive green, russet or midnight blue.

One-shape designs

One-shape designs are an excellent showcase for clever handling of color and light and shade effects. Their success relies on a good choice of fabrics and the ability to keep seams aligned. Using papers (p. 20) helps toward accuracy.

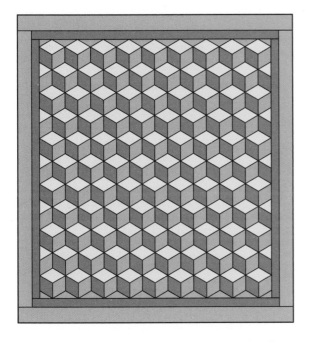

Tumbling blocks A traditional design using equal quantities of light, medium and dark fabrics in a repeat pattern that creates the illusion of falling blocks. The wide diamond template (which essentially consists of two equilateral triangles) has an acute angle of 60 degrees and a wide angle of 120 degrees. The piecing sequence can be done cube by cube; join them in rows or columns.

Mennonite sunburst Another traditional design, demanding close attention to cutting and sewing. This one is definitely for experienced stitchers. The long diamond template has an acute angle of 45 degrees and a wide angle of 135 degrees (p. 17). Each segment consists of 49 diamonds joined at the center with an eight-seam join (p. 23).

Log cabin

The most famous of all patchwork patterns, *Log Cabin* is popular for its sheer simplicity. Strips of close-woven fabric are sewn around a central square to form a larger square. No templates are needed and it can be hand- or machine-sewn, either in a single layer or attached to some type of backing. *Log Cabin* has many variations, both in piecing and arrangement of blocks, but common to all is the diagonal contrast between light and dark. By tradition, a central red square represents the hearth.

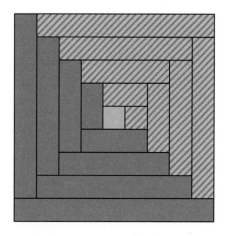

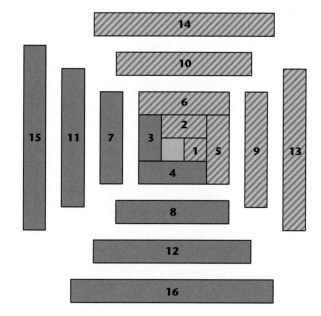

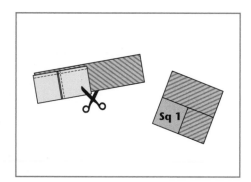

1 Prepare strips with a rotary cutter. Include ¼ in [6 mm] seam allowance on either side.

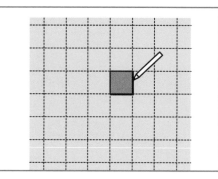

2 Mark fabric with a central square for each block and cut out with care.

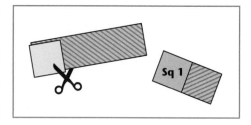

3 RS together with a ¼ in [6 mm] seam allowance, stitch first light strip to square. Trim strip to same width as square and press seam toward center.

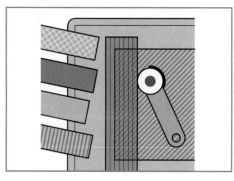

4 Attach second light strip and cut to length of previous strip plus square. Press.

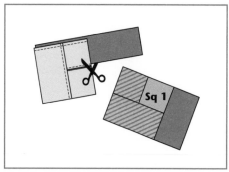

5 Take first dark strip and continue to attach counterclockwise, trimming the excess to match the pieced center. Press.

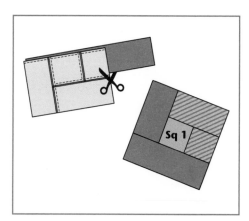

6 Attach second dark strip, trimming the excess to match pieced center as before. Press. Continue with sequence of lights and darks until block is complete.

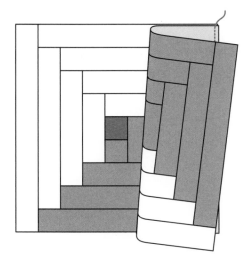

Press finished blocks carefully and check they are square. Trim if necessary, using cutting mat and ruler. All blocks must be the same size and square if the overall pattern is to work properly. Sew blocks together edge to edge in your chosen *Log Cabin* pattern.

Sunshine and shadow

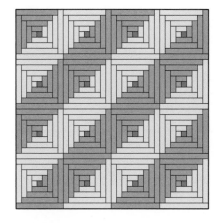

Furrows

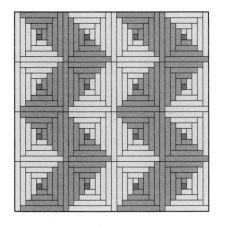

Lightning Streak

Barn Raising

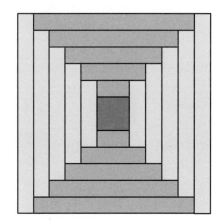

Courthouse Steps

Pressing seams

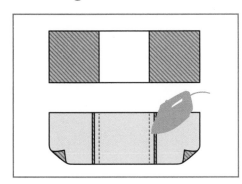

1 Patchwork seams are always pressed to one side—not open as in dressmaking—and toward the dark fabric if possible (see also p. 19).

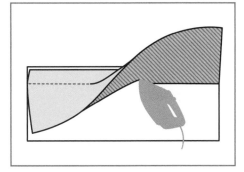

2 With a fiddly set-in or curve, press the seam open on the RS, folding the dark fabric back on itself.

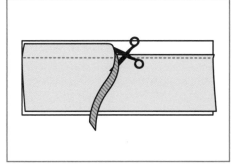

3 If you must press a seam a certain way to avoid bulk, narrow the seam allowance on the dark fabric to reduce show-through.

Curved pieces

Curved pieces are more difficult to sew than straight ones but with practice (p. 25) the results can be really impressive. The templates for *Drunkard's path* and *Double axehead* are given on p. 14.

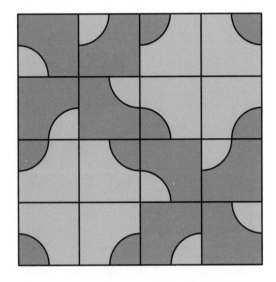

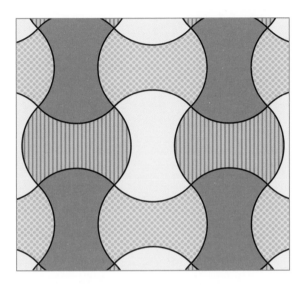

Double axehead An adaptable one-shape pattern that works on several scales. Because there are no straight lines, each and every seam must be pinned and eased, which means this pattern is more suitable for the experienced stitcher or one with a good deal of patience. Work just four patches to a block to ensure the seams lie smoothly before joining one block to the next.

Drunkard's path A two-piece patch that makes up into a 16-patch block of evenly distributed pairs. As a map of the drunkard's zigzag progress, it looks best in two plain colors; closely woven cotton being the most suitable fabric. However this pattern can be elaborated with the path picked out in a single shade, framing the remaining pieces cut from five or six other colors or prints. The result looks like stained glass.

Clamshell pattern

Silks or satins in pale pastels have a totally different character from brightly colored scrap cottons, and yet both are well suited to the shell pattern. Arrange solid colors and prints in set rows or sew them together at random. The template is on p. 14.

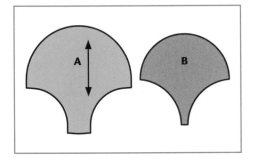

1 Trace A and B on to thin cardboard and cut fabric out using A.

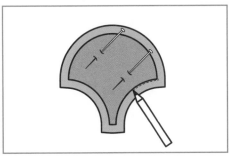

2 Pin B on to RS and outline lower curves with fabric marker.

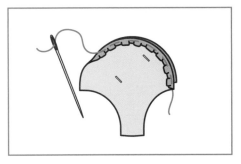

3 Turn to WS and baste small folds guided by the upper curve.

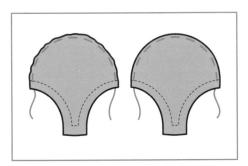

4 Remove B and press on RS to hold curve. Prepare all the shapes this way before assembling them.

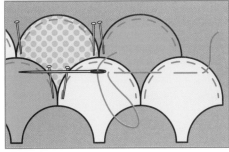

5 Pin shells in staggered rows on a sheet of cardboard, fitting upper curves to markings on lower curves. Baste together horizontally.

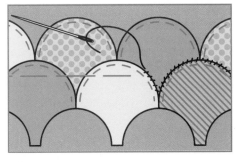

6 Unpin basted rows from board and slip stitch together around the upper curves.

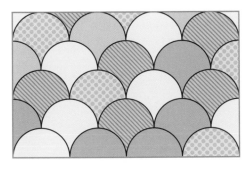

7 Remove basting]from stitched areas but not from any unstitched edges until they are finally folded and finished.

8 Using the board as in 5, turn the shells sideways. Fit upper curves into markings on lower curves and baste together before slip stitching as in 6.

Picture quilts

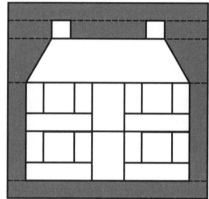

House A more complex variation on the traditional Schoolhouse block, this pattern looks good worked in solids, stripes or checks. The plan shows how to piece the block in a combination of geometric shapes and sashing (pp. 26–7). Further variations are easy to work out on graph paper.

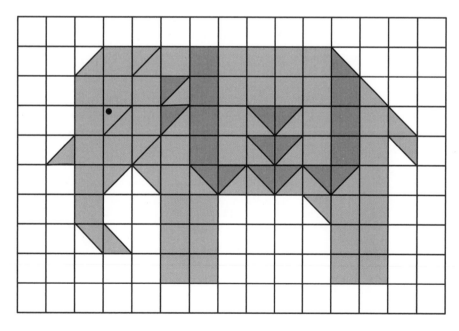

Elephant As this plan shows, an elephant can be simply but effectively pieced from squares and triangles. As a finishing touch, why not appliqué the eye, toenails and a fringed tail (p. 42)? Use graph paper to draft other animal, fish or bird shapes from squares and triangles. Make them big and bold; they look great on a child's quilt.

PART THREE:
ASSEMBLING THE QUILT

A BASIC BORDER

The edging around a quilt top can be quite plain (pp. 39–40) or worked as intricately as the top pattern itself (p. 19). It can also be used, like sashing (pp. 26–7), to harmonize with the colors that it frames.

This border consists of four strips with no mitring at the corners. Cut to any width, it can be used to increase the overall quilt size without making extra patchwork.

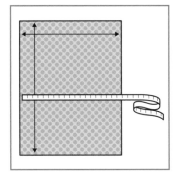

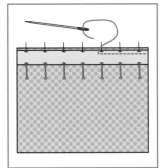

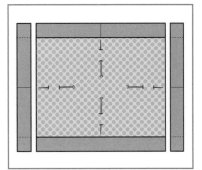

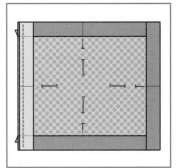

1 Measure across the middle in both directions. Cut four border strips, including a ¼ in [6 mm] seam allowance. Cut two to the length of the patchwork; the other two to the same width plus that of two border strips (see 3).

2 Take the lengthways strips first. Pin RS together to the mid-point, then outward to either end. Baste firmly before stitching. Press.

3 Line up the shorter strips, pin and baste to the main piece as in 2.

4 Sew remaining strips straight across the ends of the first two, to form a square joint. Press.

ASSEMBLY

Inserting batting

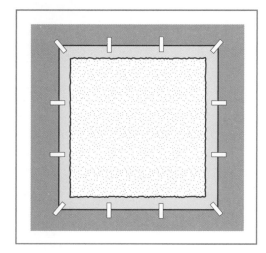

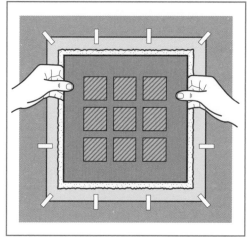

1 Press any seams in a pieced lining (p. 10). WS up, tape it to a flat surface. Center batting with a margin all round.

2 Having pressed the quilt top quite flat and made sure it is square, place RS up over the batting.

Pinning and tacking layers

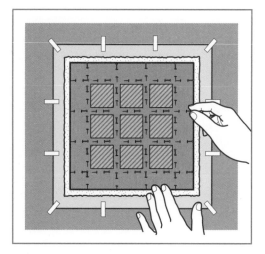

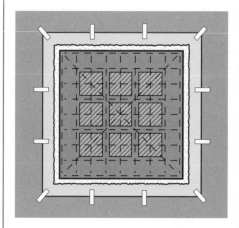

1 Pin all three layers together with long straight pins or large safety pins. You will need plenty for this stage.

2 Knot the thread end and, starting at the center, baste out toward the edges. First, stitch horizontally and vertically at 4 in [10 cm] intervals; then from the center diagonally to each corner.

Machine quilting

For quilts too thick to hand-stitch: load the machine with No 40 cotton and a new 14 needle; set the stitch length to ten per 1 in [2.5 cm]. Choose a top thread that blends with your patchwork, and wind two bobbins with a color to match the lining. *Do not use hand quilting thread*, as it has a wax coat that interferes with the machine's tension discs.

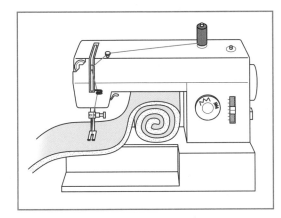

1 Roll the quilt tightly at one end and tuck under the machine throat. Begin parallel lines of stitching at the halfway point along one edge. Start and finish each line with forward and reverse stitches.

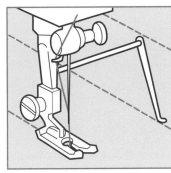

2 If you have one, use a walking/quilting foot (p. 11). A spacer guide usefully sets a regular interval between stitch lines.

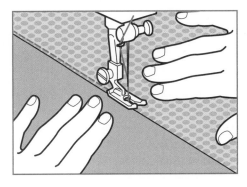

3 Don't drag the quilt as you sew – this causes skipped stitches. Smooth fabric either side of the needle and go at a steady speed. Check the back for loops or puckers at the end of each line.

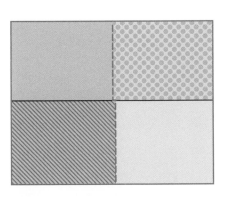

4 Ideally, seams should match but you can jump a small difference across a join when "stitching in the ditch" (when quilting follows the seams of the patchwork).

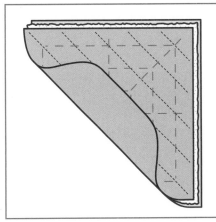

5 Roll the quilt diagonally if sewing diagonal lines. Begin at the halfway point as in 1.

Hand quilting

Baste the quilt layers together (p. 36). Hand quilters often use a frame or hoop, although many work without. Wear a metal or leather thimble on the middle finger of your sewing hand. Thread a size 8 or 10 betweens needle with wax-coated hand quilting thread, knotted at one end.

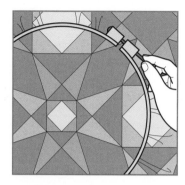

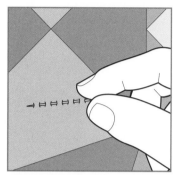

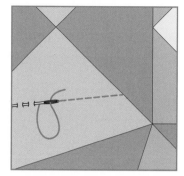

1 A quilting hoop has two rings. Separate them and lay the quilt over the inner ring. Drop the outer one over the stretched fabric and tighten the screw.

2 With one hand below the quilt for guidance, sew a series of even running stitches (p. 21) from the top. Push the head of the needle with your thimble while rocking the tip up and down through the layers.

3 Pull the thread taut to define the stitch line. If the needle is hard to pull through, grip it with a deflated toy balloon.

Tufted quilting

Tufted quilting is a quick way of securing layers that needs no basting. The tufts can look very attractive: for example, you could use two colors of knitting yarn knotted together, embroidery floss or even buttons.

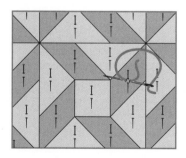

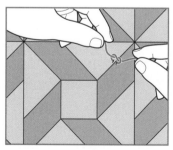

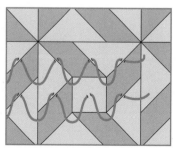

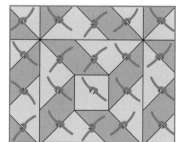

1 Mark tuft positions with long pins. Single back stitch around each pin and cut the thread.

2 Tie the free ends in a double knot and trim level.

3 Alternatively, link all the back stitches with generous loops.

4 Cut the loops and knot each pair of ends over the central stitch.

FINISHING

Fold-over edge

This is the simplest finish of all. Trim top, batting and lining level all round. Together, fold the lining fabric and batting back 5/8 in [15 mm]. Pin or baste to hold them in position if necessary. Turn top edge under once to meet folded edge of lining. Slip stitch top and lining together.

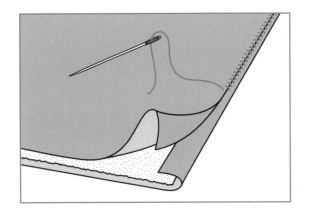

Self-bound edge

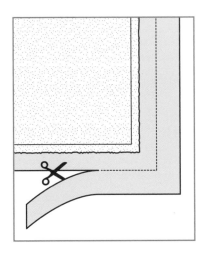

1 With top and batting already trimmed level, cut lining with an allowance of 1–2 in [2.5–5 cm] all round.

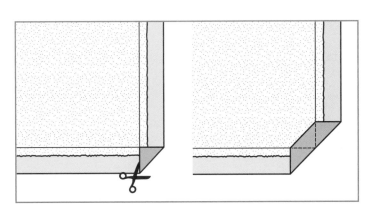

2 Fold, cut and fold again each corner of the lining, in preparation for mitring.

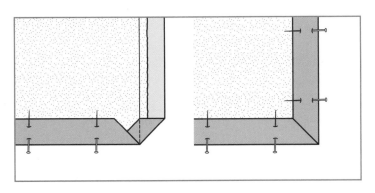

3 Fold the lining upward to meet the quilt top and form a self-binding. Turn raw edges under and pin adjacent sides, with corners meeting in a neat diagonal line.

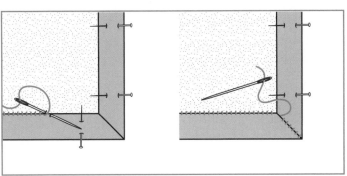

4 Using matching thread, slip stitch the binding to the quilt top all round, closing each mitred corner as you go.

Straight bound edge

Measure quilt both ways and add 2 in [5 cm] to length and width. On the grain (p. 8), cut four binding strips 1½–2 in [3.8–5 cm] wide. Press a turning of ¼ in [6 mm] down one side of each strip.

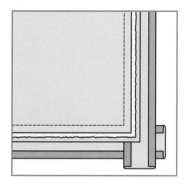

1 RS together, align unturned edge with raw edge of quilt top. Machine stitch together with a ¼ in [6 mm] seam allowance. Prepare all four sides like this.

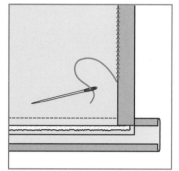

2 Fold pressed edge of binding over to WS. Pin and slip stitch first length to lining fabric, covering initial stitch line.

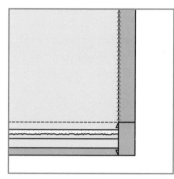

3 Fold in edge of adjacent binding. Trim away bulk if necessary.

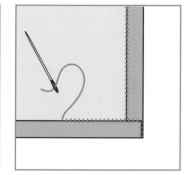

4 Fold binding up to cover all raw edges. Slip stitch to lining fabric as in 2 and close squared corner. Repeat around quilt.

Bias bound edge

Bias binding is often used on quilted items that cannot be neatened by turning. It can be homemade from steam-pressed bias strips to your chosen width, or bought readymade in various widths and materials.

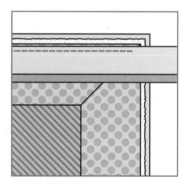

1 Press open one side of the bias binding. RS together, align with raw edge of quilt top. Pin and stitch along fold line of binding.

2 Carry on sewing right round the quilt. The bias (p. 8) will stretch around the corners as shown on the *Rose of Sharon* quilt opposite.

Signing your quilt

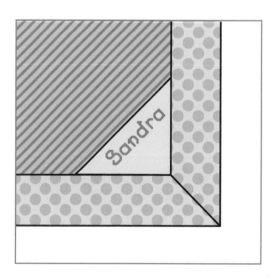

As a finishing touch, embroider your name and the date on to the quilt. Work it into the border, or make a separate label that can be slipstitched to the lining or bound neatly into one corner, as shown here.

PART FOUR:
APPLIQUÉ AND QUILTING

APPLIQUÉ

Appliqué means applied and describes the technique of stitching one fabric on top of another, either by hand or machine. Practical and decorative, it is widely used on clothes and soft furnishings. As a fabric art, appliqué goes back to the Ancient Egyptians and is now firmly established among quiltmakers.

The *Rose of Sharon* pattern frequently appeared on American bridal quilts. Complex appliqué like this involves careful planning; the plans show the stitching order for the rose motif. Repeat shapes are cut from paper or cardboard templates, based on original drafts on graph paper. When it is finished, always press appliqué RS down on a padded surface.

Rose of Sharon block

Border

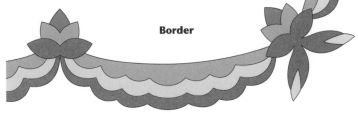

Cutting out and attaching appliqué

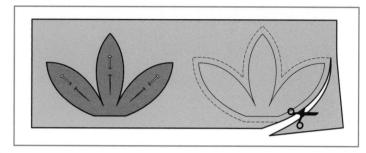

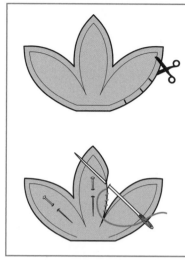

1 Pin template to fabric and trace round with a fabric marker. Cut shape out with ¼ in [6 mm] seam allowance; omit allowance if planning to oversew (3).

2 Make small clips on curves for a smooth edge when slip stitching appliqué to base fabric (p. 21). With size 8 sharps needle and waxed quilting thread, turn seam allowance under with needle tip as you sew.

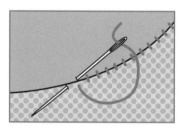

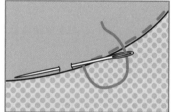

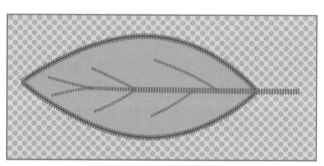

3 You can oversew the raw edges of your shape directly on to the base fabric. Sew stitches close together if the edges fray.

4 Running stitch can be used for attaching non-fraying material such as felt.

5 Appliqué by machine offers a wide choice of stitch effects, including zigzag and satin stitch.

Outlining with braid and cord

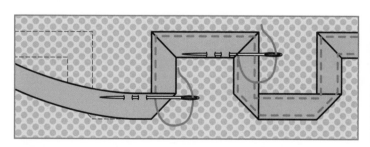

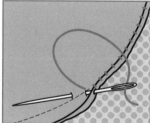

1 Add emphasis to applied shapes by outlining them. Braid may be sewn on by hand or machine; however, it must be done with precision and no wrinkles.

2 Cord defines curves where braid cannot. It is couched down by hand sewing. The needle passes through the cord and picks up threads at the edge of the appliqué, pulling the two together.

Hawaiian appliqué

A formalized style of appliqué, where intricate designs are cut from folded paper and transferred to a plain colored fabric. The fabric is cut out and sewn onto a white background. Quilting afterward outlines the pattern in multiple rows known as kapa lau.

The template starts as a square piece of paper folded in half twice and then a third time on the diagonal, which will produce eight sections. A design is drawn on one triangular section and traced on to a section of fabric folded in the same way.

With the layers of fabric pinned together, the appliqué is cut out with very sharp scissors along the traced lines. When opened, it is pinned and basted firmly to the white base fabric. Working from the center outward, the appliqué edge is rolled under by 1/8 in [3 mm] and neatly oversewn clockwise with matching waxed thread.

ANTIQUE CUT OUTS

Two mid-nineteenth-century templates cut from contemporary New York State newspapers and used to create appliquéd designs for a bridal quilt that sadly remained unfinished.

QUILTING

Quilting is the process of joining the three layers of a wadded quilt together with a stitched pattern that gives texture to a plain surface.

Quilting became a cottage industry in nineteenth-century Britain, and certain motifs—like the conical shells shown right—became stock-in-trade. Craftsmen and women set themselves up to stitch quilts for others, even taking their frames to work in customers' houses. In America, the same task gave rise to more lively social gatherings, called quilting bees.

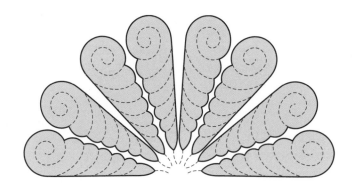

Stitching method

An introduction to hand quilting and the necessary equipment appears on p. 38.

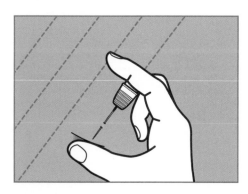

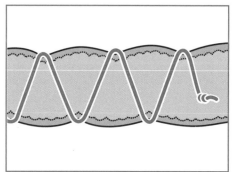

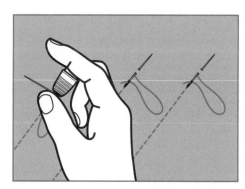

1 Following the markings, stitch rows of small, even running stitches through all three layers. In the past, rows were regularly stitched no more than 2 in [5 cm] apart to ensure the filling stayed in place.

2 Stitches will get smaller with practice. Few achieve the ideal of ten stitches per inch [2.5 cm]; six is more realistic. Pull the thread taut enough to make indentations in both surfaces.

3 To help work evenly across a large quilt, it's a good idea to have several needles threaded up at once.

Some traditional stitched details

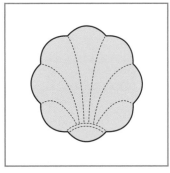

1 An Amish roundel and quilt border pattern (p. 28).

2 A scallop shell motif from Northumberland, in north-east England.

3 A Jacobean-style corner piece, reminiscent of crewel embroidery.

A CORDED EDGE

Cording, sandwiched securely between the top and backing fabric, gives a neat, firm edge to finely stitched quilting. The cord itself should be pre-shrunk. It comes in various sizes; use the one appropriate for your fabric. Cording must be supple enough to bend around corners and so it is encased in bias-cut strips.

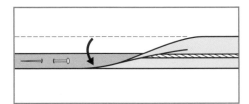

1 Pin the cord into the bias-cut strip and baste, leaving a ⁵⁄₈ in [15 mm] seam allowance.

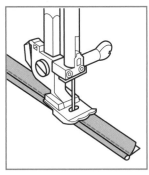

2 Machine stitch as close as possible to the cord. Use a cording or zipper foot for best results.

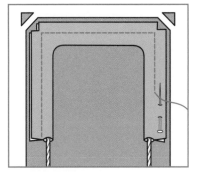

3 Raw edges aligned, baste and machine stitch cording around RS of quilt top, ends overlapping ⁵⁄₈ in [15 mm]. Trim bulk to give neatly turned corners. Fold raw edges inward so cord stands proud. Turn in raw edges of the backing to just below curve of cord. Slip stitch folded edge of backing to the cording fabric.

SASHIKO

The Japanese embroidery Sashiko lends itself to quilting because it uses a long running stitch. Around three centuries ago, Japanese men wore indigo-dyed jackets constructed from two layers of fabric. The women stitched these layers together for durability, and so the familiar Sashiko patterns evolved.

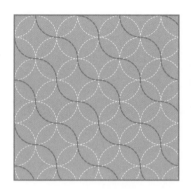   
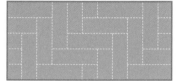

Here are five traditional Sashiko designs: horizontal and vertical lines are usually stitched first and then the diagonals; any remaining shapes are done last. Sashiko needles are 2 in [5 cm] long with a uniform shaft. The stitch count is five or six to an inch [2.5 cm]. Use thick white thread—such as pearl embroidery twist—on dark blue cotton fabric for an authentic look.

This quilted purse uses a Sashiko pattern that includes decorative glass beads.

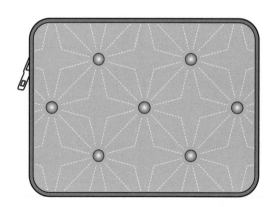

DISPLAY AND AFTERCARE

Display

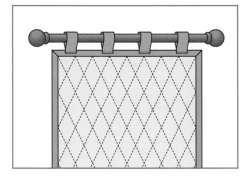

To display your work as a wall hanging, maybe in an exhibition, you must have some way of suspending it. Construct a row of tabs from fabric that matches the quilt border. Oversew the base of each tab firmly to the fabric backing, or attach with strips of Velcro so that you can easily re-convert the quilt into a bed cover. Sew the soft, looped half of the Velcro to the quilt itself, and sew the hooked half to the tab.

Any unframed fabric that is not behind glass will inevitably collect dust, which in turn can attract damp and insect pests. Vacuum clean your hangings regularly and take them down to shake outdoors from time to time. Small samplers of finely stitched quilting can be box framed to keep them clean. A roundel of Welsh or Amish design, quilted on plain fabric, shows up beautifully with the right light on it.

Aftercare

Look for the care symbols on any fabric that you buy; the manufacturer's care label appears on the bolt and if possible, ask for a care ticket to take away with you. Other points of reference are your own washing machine and dryer manuals. These give details of all the washing and drying programs.

Synthetic batting is machine washable and can be tumble dried; make certain the quilt top and backing can be treated the same. On the other hand, cotton batting should always be pre-shrunk unless you want an antique effect—some quilters use it straight from the roll deliberately because when they wash the finished quilt, it will dry with a puckered appearance typical of the quilts of the past.

If you have lightweight woolens or silk in your patchwork, and you want to wash it either by hand or machine, choose a liquid laundry detergent for delicates. The cleansing agents in liquid soaps are designed to work at low temperatures and won't leave a powdery deposit. Test strong colors (especially reds) for colorfastness and if in any doubt dry clean the quilt. Woolen or wool-mix fabrics of any kind should always be rinsed in warm water. Use the machine-washable wool setting on your machine, not the low-temperature or hand-wash program that delivers a cold rinse.

Tumble dryers are large contributors to accidental shrinkage, and some fabrics are better left to dry without any heat at all. Lift your quilt from the washing machine

and use a clean towel to remove excess water. Lay the quilt to dry flat or drape it over a drying rack. If necessary, iron fabrics according to the recommended heat setting. Take extra care with trimmings; nylon lace, metallic threads and plastic sequins will shrivel at the touch of a hot iron.

When storing household linen, put items away clean, dry, and unstarched (silverfish love starch). Dust, dirt and perspiration harm and discolor fibers of all kinds, and both moths and molds feed readily on dirt. Keep quilts folded neatly in chests and cupboards, or inside zipped cotton covers for long-term storage. Shake them out occasionally and refold a different way to prevent permanent creases. Avoid the risk of mold or mildew by never storing fabrics in poorly ventilated, damp or humid surroundings such as lofts, cellars or neglected cupboards. Low-powered heaters and dehumidifiers help to combat damp and condensation.

While you may see clothes moths in flight if they are present in your house, it is their larvae that make the holes in fabric. There are pleasant alternatives to camphor mothballs, such as cedarwood blocks and lavender bags, although these will need to be renewed. Moths not only lay their eggs on wool but can ruin silk, fur or feathers. Check storage places regularly; keep disturbing the moths' potential habitat and they won't settle.

TERMS AND ABBREVIATIONS

Appliqué Technique of stitching one fabric on top of another

Backing The quilt lining

Basting [Tacking] Temporary stitches made with running stitch

Batting [Wadding] Padding in the center layer of a quilt

Betweens Needles for fine stitching and quilting

Bias Any diagonal line between lengthwise and crosswise grains

Block Pieced units sewn separately and later assembled into an overall pattern

Border Fabric edging or frame added to the top layer of a quilt

Fat quarter Half yard of fabric cut off the bolt then cut in half again along the lengthwise grain

Felt Non-woven fabric made from compressed fibers

Filling Padding sewn between quilt top and backing

Fusible web Iron-on synthetic bonding material

Grain Direction in which the warp and weft threads lie

Hem Folded and stitched edge, to prevent fraying

Isometric paper Paper printed in a grid of equilateral triangles

Latticing Narrow strips used to separate quilt blocks. Also called sashing

Mitre Corner pieces joined at an angle of 45 degrees

Muslin Translucent loose-woven cotton fabric

Nap Texture or design that runs in one direction only

Notch Small triangular cut-outs in the seam allowance, for aligning pieces when sewing

Patch A shaped piece of fabric

Patchwork Fabric shapes or patches sewn together in a set design

Pearl thread Cotton embroidery twist

Piecing Joining fabric shapes or patches together

Pile Soft raised surface on velvet, corduroy etc. (see Nap)

Post Small square connecting sashing/lattice strips

Press Often used to mean iron but more strictly involves steam and a pressing cloth

Presser foot Holds fabric flat while the machine needle makes stitches

Quilt Bed cover consisting of two layers of fabric with padding sewn or tied between

Quilting Action of stitching the three layers of a quilt together

Quilting hoop Portable frame for holding a portion of quilt while stitching

RS Right side of fabric

Rotary cutter Cuts strips and several layers of fabric at once.

Sashiko Traditional Japanese type of embroidery

Sashing Narrow strips used to separate quilt blocks. Also called latticing

Seam allowance Distance between the cut edge and the seam line

Seam ripper Tool for removing machine stitching

Selvage Solid edge of a woven fabric

Seminole Strip-pieced technique often used for borders

Setting in Fitting one piece into an angle formed by two others already joined

Sharps General sewing needles

Slip stitch Attaches a folded edge to a flat surface

String Technique of creating a fabric from strips

Strip Technique of pattern building based on strips of fabric rather than blocks

Template An outline guide for tracing and cutting

Top Patterned top layer of a patchwork quilt

Tufted Method of securing quilt layers with knots of thread

WS Wrong side of fabric

Warp Runs lengthwise, parallel to the selvage

Weft Runs at right angles to the selvage